Lion's Lair

spoken word poetry

Also by
AMANI ABDUL

Lyrics of an Angel: poetry in reality

MUSE: The Lyrics

**Chasing Peace: Freeing Your Spirit and
Releasing Your Soul**

MUSE Poetry CD
www.AmaniAbdul.com
Amazon.com
iTunes
CDBaby

Lion's Lair

by Amani Abdul

Original Copyright © 2014
by Amani Abdul

ISBN 978-1-929985-09-8

Cover design by Frankie Fultz

For orders or information, write to:
info@AmaniAbdul.com

www.AmaniAbdul.com

Angel Heart Publishing

Dedicated in Loving Memory of
my Dear Friend, M.T.C.

My Best Friend:
"You were my friend, yes, one of many,
but you were the best and
now I haven't any."

Rest In Peace.

Love Always & Forever.

POEMS

-ROAR-

because of my mouth
one less brotha to deal with
marc
unwrap yourself
i wish
reflection
who the f are they?

-DEN-

boundaries
captured
magnificent
ken
constant deception
contradiction
how
feeling like this
looking through the our glass
when i'm with you
lano
i dreamed of you
mr. perfection
voodoo child
rewind
linked
will my dream ever come
friday night
a loveless tale
wasted time

ROAR

BECAUSE OF MY MOUTH

because of my mouth
you'll know how I feel
because of my mouth
what I say is real
because of my mouth
I speak the truth
because of my mouth
I'm trying to educate these youth
because of my mouth
I have the right
because of my mouth
I'm putting up a verbal fight.

ONE LESS BROTHA TO DEAL WITH

when you drop
from a smokin' guns pop
'cause you can't stop
not scared of no cop
YOU'RE JUST A STATISTIC
One Less Brotha To Deal With!

when you feel as if you're about to fail
end up in the county jail
can't make bail
no one sendin' you any mail
YOU'RE JUST A STATISTIC
One Less Brotha To Deal With!

when you're high as the sky
life's just passin' you by
while your livin' a lie
'cause you think you're that guy
YOU'RE JUST A STATISTIC
One Less Brotha To Deal With!

when you find yourself walking around
with a frown
'cause everyone let you down
been stripped of your only crown
'cause your skin is brown
YOU'RE JUST A STATISTIC
One Less Brotha To Deal With!

DON'T LET ANYONE ROB YOU OF YOUR
POTENTIAL FOR GREATNESS!

MARC

When I speak
I don't expect for you to listen
although I would like for you
to understand
I'm not one for dissin'
but you're such an impeccable young man.

Don't want you to get caught up
in life's sweet luxuries
I understand that sometimes were taught
that's the way it should be.

I see something in you
that once was in me
tryin' to live for that almighty dollar
tell me… *Is it really that mighty?*

I know that you want the best
that is quite understood
but are you willing
to put your life to the test
Is the money all that good?

You have such potential
you possess such great gifts
what talent to waste with no credentials
as your life will continue to drift.

I believe in you
and your ability to succeed
do what you need to do,
not what you have to or want to

don't get sucked in by greed.

Tomorrow is never promised
no matter what type of life you lead
but it's no reason to speed
your chances of survival
and become another statistic of your creed.

UNWRAP YOURSELF

Death has been my shadow
since the age of sixteen
followed me wherever I go
and was always seen
my friends droppin' all around me
like an action movie
playing on the silver screen
death was on their ground
and with me stayed in between.
I'm sure I was spared for a reason
maybe to preach my word
everyone has a duty, a job
a gift to give, for God must be heard.
Once above you'll be judged
on the life you have lived..
What have you put back
of all that you took?
What to this world did you give?
Everything you've done
was already written for you
all you had to do is live,
everyone has a talent that they possess
or mission to complete
but few see it
and choose to neglect their gift.
God has given you a reason for your walk
but all you have to do is see it through
Unwrap Yourself, shed this world
because your present lies dormant
within you.

I WISH

I wish I could love you
…and take the pain away
I wish I could hold you
…and tell you everything's going to be
okay
I wish I could help you
…to forget all your troubles of yesterday
I wish I could promise you
…that there will be a better way
I wish I could join you
…into the dawn of a brand new day
So I wish the best for you
…forever, starting today.

REFLECTION

as I look into your eyes
an activist I see
a true revolutionary

as I look into your eyes
I see your constant misery
wishing I could find a way to set you
forever free

as I look into your eyes
I feel your pain run through me
Why do I feel so close?
when I look into the mirror…
Why is it YOU I see?

as I look into your eyes
I see your masked emotions
How do I bring them out?
please give me a notion

as I look into your eyes
I feel you getting near
What do I do?
Why this feeling do I fear?

because it is when I look into your eyes
I see *ME*
again
ever so clear.

WHO THE HECK ARE they?

Who The Heck Are they?
they sure have a lot to say
I stay in dismay
Wondering …
Who The Heck Are they?

People come to me
telling me what they've heard
from "them" and "they"
How can one take their word?
or believe what they say
when they might be telling a fraction of a
truth
composed of a full lie
acting like infants and youths
and because of them, at times we have to
say goodbye.

Who The Heck Are they?
Why can't I know their name?
When in front of me they pose a different
array
and behind my back they play with my life
a game.

JEALOUSY: is an awful thing,
RUMORS: grief to your life they bring,
but that's the way the HATERS swing;
"LIES" is the name of the songs that they
sing.

"they" said,

U heard…
out on the street
yet another word--
from "them" and "they" once again,
trying to break me away from an
acquaintance, associate, or even a friend.

So Who in The Heck Are they?
When in my business they like to stay,
and in my love life they tend to play,
and from me knowing who the heck they
are
they like to get away!
WHO THE HECK ARE they???

CUT-
A friend once told me that *they*
don't talk about just anybody,
they always talk about somebody.
And *they*, the majority
of the time are nobody,
trying to take from somebody.
So I guess I'm doing something right.
Keep on talking and saying nothing.

DEN

BOUNDARIES

am i to blame 4 what i feel inside
when i catch your eyes
staring into mine
i c u looking through me
once again my emotions get caught
feelings cross
boundaries lost

how long can i cover it
i hold on and hide
lying in confusion
standing twisted
awkward this seems 2 me
my boundaries i can't c

i feel your gentle touch
your tenderness brings me close
oh why must i feel like this
thoughtless
full of passion
my boundaries have come crashin'

CAPTURED

Am I still bound?
for whatever reason
I keep you around
up and down
this merry-go-round
nothing to be said
nothing to be found
yet my heart still lies
on your very own ground.

MAGNIFICENT

This feeling that he gave to me
had me
translucent
around him
allowing his mind to penetrate
through
waves of solitude
that I once had
in wonderment I would
stare at him
as he speaks
made my knees weak
coincidence?
I think not
have I hit the jackpot
oh, what have I got
myself into this time
as I connect from dot to dot
through rhythm and rhyme
but what
was
is
his intent
or is it evident
that this was all immanent
a fragment of my supernatural element
I thought it was Magnificent.

As he was dissident
more eminent
than anyone I had met
and only he

would be
able to see
through
with words
it was me
he drew
at the breakfast table
could it be true
is it possible
for me
to stay in constant merriment
with you
I thought it was Magnificent.

And in time our knowledge
for one another
will grow
through a more
substantial
light of glow
that will exceed
with more information
to feed
the other
hoping to realize
a deeper need
more profound greed
together-meant
I thought *he* was
Magnificent.

KEN

You tell me that you love me
you say that you care
but in our time together
I always wondered if you were there

You talk about our future
you swear your love is true
but as time passes on
I wondered why you'd leave me blue

I questioned was I happy
I questioned if I'd ever be
I wondered if in time
you'd stop deceiving me

My heart said you were the one
to love eternally
but my head disagreed
and said you couldn't hardly be

I believe time will show
if we were meant to be
and if not, then I will go
and set you forever free.

CONSTANT DECEPTION

It was wonderful
when it all began
never would have believed
in bitterness this will end
in constant deception
we're beginning to lay
while your contradictions
keep me in dismay
What happened to our happiness?
Where has it gone?
as we sit in loneliness
awakened by the dawn.

CONTRADICTION

why do you stay
when there's no chance
continue to pray
and still no romance

are you giving too much
and therefore expecting a lot
is there such a thing
or maybe not

you hear what he's saying
often you already know
contradicting and delaying
yet, you want to believe in him so

deep in thought
you continue to be
you're feelings get caught up
waiting to see

it would be nice
if everything worked out
you wish he were more precise
and alleviated your doubt

so you choose to sit back
and watch for every clue
hoping your assessment
will conclude he's true.

HOW

how could one who once made me laugh
now make me cry
how could one whom you loved
make you want to say goodbye
how could one disturb your world
and place you in misery
how could one make a fool of you
how could this be?

FEELING LIKE THIS

…Tell me…
What would have happened
if you would have stayed?
Do you think we would have
continued to have played?
How far would we have went?
Is it my juices flowin'
you would have sent?
Could I really be
Feeling Like This?
Would we always be satisfied
with a hug and kiss?
When your away
is it you that I should miss?
Should I really be
Feeling Like This?
As I think about your sweet touch…
and try to explain
why you're on my mind so much
I make believe there can't be no thing as
such
As I speak of my more than a crush…
Say now…
It seems that I can't resist
is it any wonder
why I'm
Feeling Like This?

LOOKING THROUGH THE OUR GLASS

tall or short
small, medium or large
so check this out babe,
who's in charge?
Me?
You?
Who's it gonna be, boo?
What'cha puttin' me through?
I think I can see
put my glasses on
to magnify
NO!
not Me
but You
on the sly
hour by hour
makin' ideal conversation
look at us now
what a situation
as time goes by
through my eyes
I magnify
Looking Through the Our Glass
at your fine
lying ass
men are the same
no matter what
color, creed or creation
same ol' song
what a sad revelation.

WHEN I'M WITH YOU

When I'm with you,
it's like summer time in winter
or spring in fall
quiet and cold as it is
I still hear the birds mating call
with every step
my heart skips a beat or two
just as the seasons did
whenever I'm with you.

When I'm with you,
you brighten my day
whether old or new
you always take the blues away
I don't know how
I can give this feeling back
or what to do
but I can try to give it back
whenever I'm with you.

When I'm with you,
I enjoy our time
together spent
hoping you do too
fast it goes
yet it comes again
never do I
want the day to end
whenever I'm with you.

LANO

when we first met
I saw a portrait of a player
a good time swayer
funny as it may sound
I never thought
that such a cool cat
could be around
what a silly clown
pick me up
when I'm down
make me laugh
all over town
my heart's never at a frown

you're so good to me
as a friend should really be
I can see why
you may have my hearts key
and if there's anything that I
can ever do for you
just ask me
and it will be
done gladly
and though I may not let it show
I just want you to know
how much I appreciate and
care for you, Lano.

I DREAMED OF YOU

just as I thought
it could never be
here you come walking
straight in front of me
I was ready to settle
for something I thought I desired
when here comes you
the one my imagination admired
my heart jumped right out
and landed in your hand
it was then that I knew
that you had to be that man
flawless and fierce
as I dreamed you'd be
and our conversation proved
what my heart all this time could see
now as I sit back and think
of that very peculiar day
I always thank God
for bringing you my way

MR. PERFECTION

Mr. Perfection, oh where have u been
hey u! Mr. Perfection, a broken heart
won't mend
never thought I'd find you
didn't think you exist
when just right out of the blue
you stepped out the mist
stole my heart
before it hit its second beat
as others whispered
it was evident we'd meet
as you worked your way around
the whole entire place
I couldn't resist but stare
at that perfect glowing face
body of a Greek god
smile of the bright sun
an attitude well grounded
and you sure seem to be a lot of fun
oh Mr. Perfection
I've been waiting for you all this time
hey there you Mr. Perfection
breaking hearts should be a crime.

VOODOO CHILD

I don't understand the magic
within me you hold
but it's actually quite tragic
to witness its power and control
can hardly eat a bite
my eyes through the tears are burning
unable to sleep at night
cause the thought of you keeps me tossing
and turning
you give me a feeling
a vibe of pure delight
now I'm sitting here dealing
as I try to continuously fight
this is something new
I just want to comprehend
but I never meant for you
to walk away my friend
never thought I'd experience this
didn't have a clue
but now that you're at a miss
I'm just feeling more blue…
didn't mean to scare you
that was not my intention to be
I just wanted you to have a clue
of what's going on with me
I don't know who hurt you
don't know if someone has
but I'm not that person
and I thought this point we surpassed
I feel as if I'm catching the repercussions
of something in your present or past

but my dear I wish you'd ease up on the
caution
cause a true friend to you I will forever
last
so now I sit here in agony, aching
a feeling forever embedded in me
as I feel my heart slowly breaking
cause the truth in me... you just can't see
so in my heart I'll keep you
my buried treasure so rare
an experience no one can undo
for you are beyond compare
maybe our paths will cross
in another form sublime
and we can make up for the loss
that we took here, this time...

REWIND

ahh, My Sleeping Cutie
my very own Voodoo Child
wish you knew me
wish you weren't so wild
When I First Saw Your Smile
it etched a Space within me
left a scar imbedded for time
diluted my reality
the nature of this crime
maybe someday I'll be able to understand
the meaning of this fate
what caused me to lose my mind
and why I was the culprit's bait.

LINKED

I thought I had it all figured out
and out of the blue
you come about
floating emails
with subtle flirtation
shall this prevail
or will it turn into
an ordinary situation
what can I give you
what is it that you need
feeling me intensely
possessing me with greed
subtle morning emails
and unsubtle evening texts
have turned into late night phone calls
oh what a mess
I'm trembling
just sitting here
reviewing what I've just read
describing in graphic detail
what was done, what was said
through a dream you say
hundreds of miles apart
Linked
intertwined through a heavy beating heart
this is dangerous!
(I continue to write)
absolutely insane
from you my dear
I have to abstain.

WILL MY DREAM EVER COME?

Am I ever gonna fall in love?
Am I ever gonna hear the cry of a dove?
Am I ever gonna find that special one?
Tell me Lord…
Will my dream ever come?
The walls around me are empty, still, and
quiet.
But if I told a soul, they wouldn't buy it.
So I ask you Lord, why can't I try it?
I guess that's what I'm asking, please
don't deny it.
I know it happens to a numerous some.
I'm just wondering…
Will this dream of mine ever come?
Am I ever gonna feel that tender touch?
Am I ever gonna experience what I fear so
much?
Am I ever gonna find that perfect one?
Tell me Lord…
Will my dream ever come?
I dream he's around.
I know in my heart, he'll be found.
I refuse to believe he's a fantasy,
he's everywhere, he's all I see.
Wherever he will be lead the way and I
will go, lead him to me,
Chante Moore perfectly said it so.
Am I ever gonna find that genuine, special
ONE?
Tell me Lord..Will my dream ever come?

FRIDAY NIGHT

was kinda bored one night
invited over a friend
thought it would better my mood
didn't want to be hit on
no crowds for me tonight
felt like being a prude
just wanted to chill
with no frills
a relaxing moment
with someone cool
however it was myself
that got played for a fool
it turns that my friend evidently
had an agenda on his mind
can't believe that such idiots
existed of his kind
what was he thinking?
what could have been on his brain?
how could he risk such a friendship
to go down the drain?
so I guess this Friday eve
was meant for me to spend alone
and when again I feel like this
I guess I'll just stay on my own.

A LOVELESS TALE

I remember once upon a time
when I was engaged to be married
and my God parents heard the word

I was working at this store
and it was about quarter to four
an hour and fifteen minutes until closing
time
when they barged in
and spoke their minds

Even the lady down the hall
came to chime in
and they all sat there
one by one they went in

"Child,
[Emma said]
you're making a big mistake
one that you can't retake
this man, your heart he will break
this is our version of the loveless story
and our hearts ache

"See child,
[the lady from down the hall began to say]
Love is not suppose to hurt you this way
Love isn't blind
Love isn't cruel
Love is kind
and won't play you for a fool
Love is understanding, patient and sweet

Love is not one handed and won't leave
you in despair
Love won't deceive you
Love will always care
Love is passion in paradise
Love is never low
Real Love is maximized
Real Love doesn't desert or go."

WASTED TIME

it's been six years
facing my fears
shedding tears
with 2 relationships in the rear

why do I find myself in the same lame
game
trying to define, only in time
wasted, gone
wrong
relationships
with accumulated time
i stay and try
to figure things out
a better way
but why do I stay?
i'm the one unhappy here
is anyone listening?
does anyone hear me?

i wAnt out
I wAnt out
I WANT OUT

i constantly shout
action alone
can't explain my hurt
i'm suffering inside
can anyone hear me?
can they see me cry?

oh why do I get caught up in fictitious
relationships?
trying to fix grown adults

it's not my fAult
It's not My fAult
IT'S not MY fault

that these grown folks are immature
irresponsible adults
they're grown
they should have known
that no woman should settle for less

IT'S MY FAULT.

PRIDE

BUTTERFLY

a visual beauty
or feeling so great
a chameleon on duty
with a sensation you can't hate
not vain nor snooty
yet tantalizing bate
oh what a cutie
as your mesmerized by such a mate

MY DEAR FRIEND

My Dear Friend
Where have you gone?
Dear Friend
What went wrong?
I can't believe you're gone,
left me this way
never thought I'd never hear your voice
again,
when I heard it every day.

I miss you Dear Friend
and all you meant to me
Oh, my Dear, sweet Friend
where you've gone is a mystery.

I miss your warm smile
that I cherished so much
I miss your endearing hugs
and gentle touch.

Dear Friend,
Oh, how I miss your tender ways
My Dear, sweet Friend
How much I reminisce of our special days.

I MISS YOU SO MUCH...

LOVE

aching to burst
my body's on fire
mouth watering with thirst
yet never quenched desire
needing you close
wanting you near
but unlike most
it's *you*, I fear
my need to feel you
as if it may never be
don't have a clue
what's wrong with me

LONELY BUT NOT ALONE

No one knows my pain
as I strain
to remain
Strong.
Loneliness is my middle name
no one to blame
but I
because only to I
I belong.
but for how long?
Too critical of partners
all come
only for me to let them go
when will I find my
true love
no one will truly know
Me
and see
through and beyond my anonymity
however
reality hits..
As people assume
I have it all
little do they know
I'm just a made up doll
consumed
in a world
of false illusion
I'm not into any confusion
but in this destitution
I continue to stay
until that true and genuine one

comes my way.
All the fakeness
and follies
of all these wanna be partners
and colleagues
just kill me to the bone,
so until I find what's true
I'm just gonna kick it with my crew
however,
I thank God
that I
am never
alone.

MOTHER

What would I do without you?
you've given me so much
unselfishly
relentlessly
and you inspire me
to be
the best person I can
a better woman
a true giver of life
you are the ultimate
superwoman
without constant recognition
a super hero
on an everyday mission
to provide
to care for
lovingly
constantly
and completely adore
me
little ole me
how can I repay
your gratitude
continuous
unconditional love
always there to listen
to share
your wisdom
though sometimes
you know I may not listen
but always
you're there

with tender love
and care
to support
and stand beside me
Mother
I am who I am
because you have inspired me.

LOVE KNOCKS

my heart is beating faster
my stomach is tied up in knots
my breathing is so heavy
my vision has gone to specks and spots
my eyes are feeling drowsy
my mind can't figure out what to do
my body is trembling
"Hello?
Love?
… is that you?"

WILD ORCHID

luxury
hard not to be aware
luster
of pure delicate care
erotic
and
exotic
enticing you
into a psychotic dare
of lust
and passionate desire
Her luscious nature
will set
anybody's mind on fire.

MAN DOWN

if I were to tell you
would you believe
could you understand
will you be able to perceive me
would you be that man
if I were to ask you
to be around
will you adhere
would you make a sound
will you even be able to be found
when my life is upside down
if I tell you
who I am
can you comprehend
would you give a damn
will you lend to me your ears
or pretend to hear
would you protect my heart
could you mend my fears
would you collect my tears
in the moonlight
and shovel my heart out of the snow
or will you run for open waters
and leave me there, alone,
to sink further below?

LOCKED OUT

My emotions run deep
so please understand
that I can't just let some creep
or any ol' man
come
close
to
my

heart.

WHY

why be alone?
don't turn my heart into stone
why be cruel?
please don't play me for a fool
why give my heart to an ungrateful soul
why?
'cause once broken
a heart can turn cold
why bother with a situation
that can never be
do you actually think
i would let you close enough
to hurt me?